Contents

Words printed in bold letters **like these** are explained in the Glossary.

What do you need?

To go swimming boys usually wear swimming trunks and girls wear a swimming costume.

▲ **Chlorine** in the water can make your eyes sore. A pair of **goggles** will protect them.

▼ **Earplugs** are useful if you have trouble with your ears.

▲ You may be asked to wear a swimming hat, especially if you have long hair.

◄**Armbands** help you swim. You wear them on your arms. Let the air out of them a bit as your swimming gets better.

►**Floats** help you to stay up in the water. They also help you to use your legs and feet properly.

◄**Rubber rings** help you float with your feet off the bottom of the pool.

►As you get better at swimming you can try using a **mask, snorkel** and **flippers**. You may not be allowed to use them at all public pools.

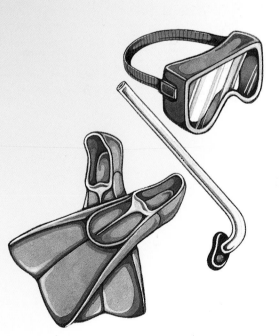

SAFETY STAR
Don't use a mask, snorkel and flippers until you can swim properly!

Is it safe?

Before you swim make sure you are safe.

Until you can swim well, only practise in water you can stand up in.

Never jump or **dive** into water until you know how deep and safe it is.

Never go swimming on your own.

➤In a public pool, read the rules and do not run around.

Don't swim in the sea if there are warning flags flying. Listen to the **lifeguards**. Never swim too far out. You may not be able to get back!

6

Think about the safety of other people, too.

Never just jump or dive in close to other people.

Never push people in.

Never jump in if you see someone in trouble, or you could be in danger too.

➤You could throw something for the person to use as a **float**. You may even find a special float nearby.

◄Use something to pull them to the side. You could use a jumper or towel for them to grab.

Are you ready?

Before you swim, make sure your body is ready by doing a **warm-up**. It helps you to do better, and stops you hurting yourself.

You must never run by a pool. But if there is somewhere nearby where you can go for a short run, this is a good way to warm up. Or try running on the spot!

These exercises make your heart beat faster and make you breathe quicker. You will also feel warmer. All of these are good for your body to get it ready for a swim.

Now you need to get your **muscles** warmed up.

The best way is to move all your **joints**. These are the parts of your body where you can bend, like your shoulders, elbows, knees and waist.

Try some **stretching** exercises as well. These make your muscles warmer and more stretchy.

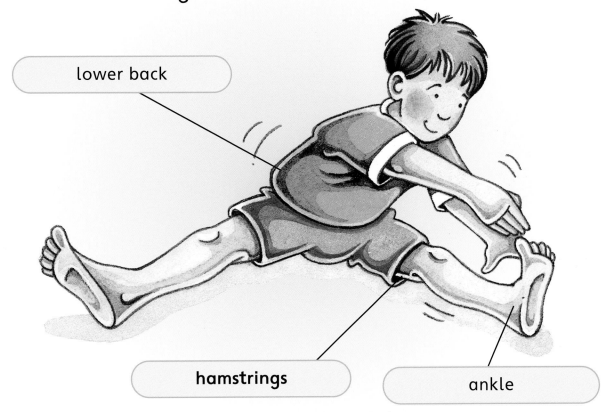

lower back

hamstrings

ankle

Now you are ready to get in the water!

Isn't water fun?

There are lots of ways of having fun while you learn to swim.

First you need to feel happy and safe in the water. Try walking around in the water to get used to it.

Next, try putting your whole body under the water.

Slide down so the water is just level with your mouth. Then lean forward and blow bubbles out into the water. It's fun!

Now try putting your whole face under the water!

Take a deep breath before you put your head under, then hold your breath and go under. Make sure you don't breathe in at all while you are underwater.

Can you open your eyes underwater? Try counting a friend's fingers when you do it.

Find some shallow water and drop something to the bottom. You could use a coin. Now try to duck down and pick it up. Always have a grown-up watching when you do this.

More things to do

Once you are used to putting your body under the water, you can try these things, too.

In shallow water, put your hands on the bottom and lift your legs up as far as you can. If you lift them high enough they will float on the top! Use your hands as feet to walk along the bottom of the pool.

Next, put your face into the water as you go along. Bob your head up and down in time to the steps you are taking with your hands.

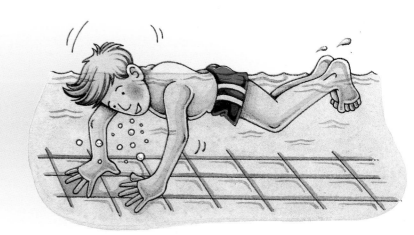

Now you are ready to go into water which is a bit deeper. Use **armbands** or a **rubber ring** at first.

Slowly walk out from shallow water to deeper water. When your feet are no longer touching the bottom, start to kick them so they move you around.

Keep practising, and you should be able to move in all directions!

See if you can lift your feet higher and higher until they are kicking at the surface behind you. Now you can really move around!

Make your legs work!

Get your legs working! Using your legs to move on your back is a great way to start. You can watch your legs and feet to make sure they are in the right place!

Put one **float** under each arm. Start off by walking backwards. Then slowly lean back until you are lying flat in the water.

Now kick your legs and feet up and down, or move them like a frog, in and out with a pushing movement. Stay as flat as you can in the water.

Now you are ready to move over onto your front.

Practise in shallow water. First, hold one end of a float tightly with two hands. Rest your arms, up to your elbows, on the float. Then lift your bottom and feet up so you are flat in the water. Now kick your feet to push yourself along!

Next, hold the float out in front of you, with your arms straight. Try putting your head down and breathing out into the water.

Moving on your tummy

Now you can practise swiming without a **float**.
Make sure that you are in shallow water.

The first **stroke** to learn is the doggy paddle. Just kick with your legs and paddle with your hands! Try to make your body really flat as you move along.

To do the front crawl, you have to lift your arms up and over to pull yourself along. Try to put your head down to breathe out into the water. It will make you flatter and you will move along better.

To do breast stroke, put your hands flat, and pull them in towards your face with your elbows up and out. Then push your hands away from you as far as you can, spread them out to the side and pull them back.

To move along, kick your legs like a frog at the same time as you move your arms. Your legs should be bent up towards your body at the same time as your hands are closest to your face.

Moving on your back

Some people find it easier to start off by swimming on their back. They can keep their face out of the water and breathe more easily. But be careful not to bump your head!

Start in shallow water. As you lean back, use your arms to keep you steady and straight.

The first **stroke** to learn on your back is called the inverted breast stroke.

Lie flat on your back in a floating position. Do the same frog-like leg kick you did for the breast stroke. Your arms should go beneath you and pull backwards, just like someone rowing a boat!

Now if you turn your body on to one side a bit, you can do the side stroke. Make long pulling movements with one arm. The other arm helps to keep your balance.

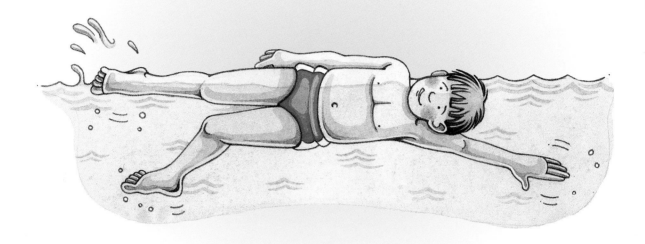

The back crawl is like the front crawl, but you do it on your back. Remember, try to get your body flat in the water. This makes it easier for you to swim.

Jumping and diving

Jumping into water is easy. Start in shallow water by just crouching down and jumping in off the side.

Once you are used to this, you can go into water which is a bit deeper. Remember, never jump into deep water unless you are a good swimmer. If you have a ring you can use it as a target to jump into.

You can start diving when you are a good swimmer.

Sit at the edge of the pool with your knees tucked up. Put your hands together and your arms out straight in front of your head.

Then roll forwards into the water. Keep your chin on your chest and let your hands and arms go in first.

As you get used to this, move from sitting to crouching and rolling in. Then slowly start higher and higher until you can do it from a standing position. Never run and dive – you may slip.

◄Diving is fun!

Keeping safe

Swimming is great fun, but to be safe you should follow all the safety tips in this book.

Every swimming pool has rules. Read them and do what they say.

If you are at the seaside there may be areas where you are not allowed to swim. Look out for warning signs and flags. Always check with a grown-up that you are swimming in a safe place.

At swimming pools and by the seaside there are usually **lifeguards**. If you are not sure about any of the rules, ask them.

Never go swimming anywhere where there is not a grown-up to look after you.

It is really dangerous to mess about. Never push other people in, and never hold them under the water.

Be very careful about how you get into water. Always check before you jump or dive in that it is safe to do so.

Don't go swimming after you have had a meal. You should wait at least an hour, or you may get pains in your stomach.

Keeping clean and safe

There are some other things you should know about when you go swimming. They are to do with **hygiene**, which means keeping clean.

Don't swim in a public pool if you have a nose or an ear **infection**.

Always use the footbaths at the pool. They contain a special **chemical**. It stops you from getting foot diseases or passing them on to other people.

Take a short shower before you get into the water. It is also a good idea to have one afterwards, to get rid of the chemicals in the pool water.

Use a clean towel to dry yourself. Make sure that all your swimming kit is washed often and kept clean.

Dry yourself carefully, especially between your toes.

Swimming is great fun but you should always be very, very, careful. Never take any risks, but remember,

YOU CAN DO IT!

Glossary

armbands blow-up bands which fit on your arms and help you stay up in the water. Never use them on your legs.

chemical substance put into the water to make it clean and safe

chlorine chemical used in pools to keep the water clean

dive way of getting into the water head first

earplugs small, plastic stoppers which stop water (which may be dirty) getting into your ears

flippers large plastic 'feet' you wear on your real feet to help you swim

float something you can use to help you to stay up in the water

goggles masks which go over your eyes so you can see more clearly underwater. They also protect your eyes from chlorine in pools.

hamstring large group of muscles at the back, top, part of your legs

hygiene keeping clean to keep you fit and healthy

infection a disease that can be passed on

joint place on your body where your bones meet and you can bend. Your shoulders and knees are joints.

lifeguard person at pools and the seaside who looks after swimmers

mask same as goggles

muscle part of your body which helps you to bend and stretch

rubber rings plastic rings which you fill with air. When you sit in the middle of them, they help you stay up in the water.

snorkel special tube which helps you breathe while you are underwater

stretching moving your muscles at the joints as much as you can

stroke way of swimming using your arms and legs

warm-up ways of moving to get your body ready for swimming

Index